CLAY SUCCULENT
GARDEN

Clay Succulent Garden

First published in the United States in 2022 by Stash Books, an imprint of C&T Publishing, Inc., P.O. Box 1456, Lafayette, CA 94549

JUSHI NENDO DE TSUKURU MINIATURE TANIKU SHOKUBUTSU
Copyright ©kitanoko 2019
All rights reserved.

Original Japanese edition published by NIHON BUNGEISHA CO., LTD.
English language rights, translation & production by World Book Media LLC, through Japan UNI Agency, Inc., Tokyo, JAPAN.

ISBN: 978-1-64403-2-299

Manufactured in China
10 9 8 7 6 5 4 3 2 1

CLAY SUCCULENT GARDEN

Sculpt 25
Miniature Plants
WITH AIR-DRY CLAY

KITANOKO

stashBOOKS®

an imprint of C&T Publishing

CONTENTS

7 | SUCCULENT PLANTS

33 | BIZARRE PLANTS

57 | PROJECT INSTRUCTIONS

There's something special about succulents—maybe it's their diminutive size or unusual shapes and colors, or maybe it's their ability to survive in the some of the harshest environments on the planet—succulents are beloved by people around the world. Yet these plants can be difficult to care for and expensive to buy, so I've created this collection of succulents crafted from clay.

The designs in this book are made with air-dry clay, which is easy to use and doesn't require baking in an oven. We'll use simple sculpting and painting techniques to capture the special features of succulents and celebrate the uniqueness of these plants.

With clay succulents, there's no need to worry about water or sunlight, so you can decorate your home with these adorable plants and enjoy their beauty stress-free!

KITANOKO

SUCCULENT PLANTS

Succulents are a group of plants with plump, fleshy leaves that store water and nutrients, allowing them to thrive in dry climates. Succulents display a variety of unique attributes, from haworthia's transparency to cacti's sharp spines. These plants possess so many special details that are perfect for capturing with clay.

SEDUM PACHYPHYLLUM

Nicknamed the jellybean plant, sedum pachyphyllum features plumply curved leaves that bear a resemblance to the candy. The leaves are a beautiful green with contrasting red tips.

Instructions: page 58

SEDUM RUBROTINCTUM

This sedum also possesses thick jellybean-shaped leaves and is known for the vibrant red coloration it develops in certain environments. Its compact appearance makes it a popular choice for potted succulent arrangements.

Instructions: page 61

SUCCULENT PLANT ARRANGEMENT

Arrange an assortment of succulents in a pot for a pretty display. Here, sedums are combined with crassula pellucida subsp. marginalis, othonna capensis, and orostachys boehmeri.

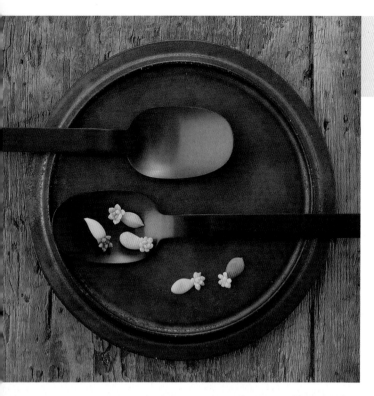

< SEDUM LEAF CUTTINGS

For a unique arrangement, display an assortment of small leaf cuttings. These colorful clippings are small yet eye-catching.

Instructions: page 63

ECHEVERIA LAUI >

This beautiful succulent features a rosette of rounded leaves that are covered in white powder. This coating is actually a wax that protects the plant from sun, rain, and insects, so you must be careful not to remove it when watering or transplanting live succulents. However, there's no need to worry with clay succulents.

Instructions: page 64

SEDEVERIA
SILVER FROST

Named for its resistance to cold weather, sedeveria silver frost has
an abundance of overlapping pointed leaves. The tips of the leaves
turn pink in the summer.

Instructions: page 66

GRAPTOPETALUM SHUUREI

This plant has thick leaves that form rosettes and vary in color from silvery-grey to pink. Without intervention, this plant will grow tall stems; however, you don't need to worry about overgrowth with clay succulents.

Instructions: page 68

< ECHEVERIA BEATRICE

This small succulent plant forms a tight rosette of silky green leaves with red or pink tips. Easy to care for, this plant is a popular choice among succulent lovers.

Instructions: page 70

LITHOPS >

Often called "living stones" for their resemblance to the rocky terrain of their natural habitat, lithops are small, interesting plants with a split hoof-like shape. Lithops adapt their colors and patterns to blend in with the stones around them and protect themselves from being eaten by animals.

Instructions: page 72

MONILARIA

Known as the bunny succulent, monilaria features long, narrow leaves that grow in pairs. When the leaves sprout, they emerge from a bubble-shaped structure at the base of the plant.

Instructions: page 74

CONOPHYTUM

This unique dwarf succulent possesses pale green bodies with transparent tips. In fact, this plant almost appears as if it's made of glass. When the plant blooms, the flowers are pale to bright pink or white with yellow stamens.

Instructions: page 76

CRASSULA PELLUCIDA SUBSP. MARGINALIS

This low-growing, spreading succulent is known for its heart-shaped green leaves with small pink spots that resemble stitches.

Instructions: page 79

ECHEVERIA
WEST RAINBOW

A colorful succulent, echeveria west rainbow features rosettes of
leaves that change color with the season. These stunning plants
exhibit shades of pink, white, purple, and green.

Instructions: page 82

< ECHEVERIA CANTE

Called the "queen of echeveria" for its renowned beauty, this plant can grow 1-2 feet wide and has thin, elegant leaves of whitish blue-green edged in rose pink.

Instructions: page 84

OTHONNA CAPENSIS >

This trailing succulent has brilliant purple or rich ruby red stems and small green leaves that resemble little pickles. When exposed to lots of sunlight, the leaves will adopt the same vibrant coloration as the stems.

Instructions: page 85

OROSTACHYS BOEHMERI

This small succulent forms open rosettes of soft, grayish green leaves.
New plants grow out of the soil on thin, spaghetti-like stems.

Instructions: page 87

HAWORTHIA 1

Succulents can be grown hydroponically, which is very stylish but more difficult as it involves checking the roots and changing the water often. With clay succulents, you don't have to worry about maintenance, you can just enjoy the cuteness of the plants!

Instructions: page 89

< HYDROPONICS

Arrange hydroponic-style clay succulents in glass vases to showcase the delicate root structure. Here, roots are added to the three varieties of haworthia showcased in this book.

Instructions: page 96

HAWORTHIA 2 & 3 >

There are over 150 varieties of haworthia, each with its own unique appearance—some have hard, spiky leaves, while others have soft, transparent "windows." Enjoy experimenting with coloration, pattern, and transparency as you recreate these plants in clay.

Instructions: pages 92 and 94

CACTI ARRANGEMENT

When arranging cacti made from clay, use sand or straw as a base. This will increase the realism and add texture.

COPIAPOA

To survive its harsh natural habitat, this cactus has developed a powdery blue-green coating that prevents against dessication. It also possesses jet black spines. This species is slow-growing and is prone to rot.

Instructions: page 98

OPUNTIA

Commonly called prickly pear, this cactus has flat paddles with large, sharp spines, as represented by the yellow dots on the clay version shown here.

Instructions: page 101

ASTROPHYTUM ASTERIAS

This species of cactus has many nicknames, including the sand dollar cactus, sea urchin cactus, and star cactus. It's known for its small round shape and white dot pattern.

Instructions: page 103

PROJECT INSPIRATION:

PHOTO FRAMES

Clay succulents make for beautiful floral arrangements, but you aren't limited to a pot when it comes to display! You can also use clay succulents to create interior decor for your home. Glue an assortment of clay succulents to a store-bought frame for one-of-a-kind wall art. Add bits of moss and straw to fill in any gaps and create a balanced arrangement.

Photo: Kitanoko

BIZARRE PLANTS

This collection of plants features some more unique species, from the popular Venus flytrap to air plants like tillandsia. Discover special sculpting and painting techniques to capture the special appearance of these plants.

TILLANDSIA
1, 2 & 3

Tillandsia are commonly known as air plants because they are able to grow on rocks, tree branches, and even telephone wires! Their leaves absorb water and nutrients, so the plants do not need soil.

Instructions: pages 105-109

MINIATURE TILLANDSIA

For added cuteness, try making the tillandisa even smaller. Have fun arranging assorted varieties to create displays.

DYCKIA

Dyckia are known for their long, pointed leaves with sharp spines along the edges. Dyckia are available in a variety of shapes, sizes, and colors, including silver and the earthy red hue pictured here. Although they are not technically succulents, dyckia are drought tolerant and easy to grow, making them popular houseplants.

Instructions: page 110

PACHYPODIUM

With their thick, spiny trunks, pachypodium look like cacti, but have leaves. These plants have large, fibrous roots that can absorb water quickly, which is necessary to take advantage of the rare rainstorms in their natural habitat.

Instructions: page 113

DIONAEA MUSCIPULA

Commonly known as the Venus flytrap, this carnivorous plant possesses tiny sensory hairs on the inner surfaces of its leaves. When insects or spiders touch the sensors more than once within 20 seconds, the leaves snap shut to trap the prey.

Instructions: page 115

PLATYCERIUM

Also known as staghorn, platycerium are ferns that grow along tree trunks. The plant possesses two types of fronds: kidney-shaped ones that grow flat against the tree trunk to protect the fern's roots from damage, and antler-shaped ones that jut out and bear spores.

Instructions: page 117

AGAVE

There are many different types of agave, each with its own pattern and color variation. This example features a rosette of thick leaves with a white brushstroke pattern. Combine different colors of clay to achieve the desired shading.

Instructions: page 120

BLACK-SPINED AGAVE

This medium-sized agave is known for its thick, pale blue-green leaves that grow in a beautiful rosette shape. The small dark teeth that grow along the edges and sharp spines at the end of the leaves provide a striking contrast.

Instructions: page 123

page 87

page 58

page 103

page 61

page 101

page 98

ACTUAL SIZE GUIDE

One of the benefits of making clay succulents is that you can customize your designs. You can change the size or shape of the succulent to fit with a particular planter or display case you have on hand. The clay succulents pictured here are photographed at actual size. Use this as a reference and make adjustments to your clay succulent creations accordingly.

page 70

page 85

page 68

page 64

page 84

page 89

page 92

page 72

page 74

page 76

page 113

page 110

page 123

page 120

page 117

page 105

CLAY SUCCULENT DETAIL GALLERY

For realistic-looking clay succulents, I recommend studying living plants or photographs to observe how the leaves change colors, where the shadows fall, and other small details. On the following pages, you'll find some additional clay succulents I've made over the years. I hope you find these images inspiring and helpful when creating your own designs!

DYCKIA

The coloration of this plant varies depending on the angle, lighting, or time of day.
It's very helpful to observe a live dyckia plant before painting the leaves.

SEDUM PACHYPHYLLUM

Round, plump leaves make this plant popular among succulent enthusiasts. Here, I've exaggerated the round shape to emphasize the cuteness.

MONILARIA

When creating the root base of the monilaria, I mixed white paint with a bit of liquid clay to create dimension. Incorporate different sizes to capture the natural look of growing roots.

< ECHEVERIA CANTE

AGAVE >

MATERIALS & TOOLS

AIR-DRY CLAY FORMULA

Air-dry clay: Lightweight air-dry clay = 3:1

All of the projects in this book were made using a mixture of air-dry clay and lightweight air-dry clay at a 3:1 ratio. When you see the word "clay" listed in the materials list for a project, use this mix, unless otherwise noted. This mixture of air-dry clay takes a few days to dry fully. Note that sculptures made from this type of clay will shrink up to 10% when dry and that the colors will dry darker.

AIR-DRY CLAY

As its name suggest, air-dry clay does not need to bake in an oven to harden. Opt for high-quality air-dry clay made from grain powder to produce sculptures with a smooth texture and finish. This type of clay displays strength and elasticity, making it ideal for forming delicate leaves. It can be blended with other colored clay or with paint. Modena and Grace brand air-dry clay were used for the projects in this book. Refer to the resources section on page 128 for suppliers.

LIGHTWEIGHT AIR-DRY CLAY

This lightweight version of air-dry clay weighs about half as much as its traditional counterpart. It has a fine texture, but is not very strong, so it works well when combined with regular air-dry clay.

TRANSPARENT AIR-DRY CLAY

This type of air-dry clay is white when it first comes out of the package, but becomes transparent when it dries. Transparent clay takes up to 10 days to fully dry and shrinks 15%-20%. Sukerukun brand transparent air-dry clay was used in this book.

VARNISHES & SEALERS

You can use varnishes and sealers to seal your air-dry clay projects and give them a shiny, semi-transparent finish—just apply after the clay dries. This is especially useful for translucent plants like haworthia. A Japanese brand of varnish made specifically for clay is pictured above, but you can also use artists' varnishes like Liquitex. Look for one with a glossy finish for best results.

AIR-DRY CLAY PASTE

This is a liquid version of air-dry clay that can be mixed with acrylic paint to create a colored paste. Use the colored paste to add dimensional spots or patterns to your clay succulents. Modena Paste air-dry clay paste was used in this book.

Before drying   *After drying*

WORKING WITH AIR-DRY CLAY

- Knead the air-dry clay when you first remove it from the package. This is known as conditioning and will make the clay easier to handle and prevent cracks from forming.

- If the clay cracks as you are shaping it, simply knead it and then re-shape as desired.

- Note that colored clay will appear darker when dry. Keep this in mind when adding color to clay (refer to page 55 for more tips).

- Air-dry clay typically shrinks down 10%-20% when dry. This will vary based on the brand.

- Once you remove the clay from the package, it dries out very quickly, so it's best to remove only the amount you plan to use. Keep the rest of the clay covered in plastic wrap and stored in a plastic bag. Keep in mind that clay that has been mixed with paint tends to dry out quicker.

- Air-dry clay takes 3-4 days to dry fully, while transparent air-dry clay can take up to 10 days.

OTHER MATERIALS & TOOLS

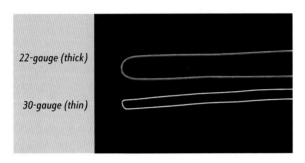

WIRE

You'll need wire to create plant stems. 22-gauge (thick) and 30-gauge (thin) wire were used for the projects in this book. Use diagonal cutting pliers to cut wire.

ACRYLIC PAINT

Mix acrylic paint with air-dry clay to create dynamic custom colors. Refer to page 55 for instructions on adding color to clay.

TOOTHPICKS: Often used for plant stems, but can also be used to apply paint to sculptures.

PLASTIC WRAP: Wrap unused clay in plastic wrap to prevent it from drying out.

CLAY WORK MAT: Use a mat to protect your work surface. If you don't have a work mat, a plastic folder is a good substitute.

GLUE: Opt for a PVA glue, such as white glue or wood glue, that dries transparent.

RULER: Use to measure the size of your clay succulent components. It's also helpful to have a circle template.

SPONGE: Use to help smooth out the clay.

MAKEUP SPONGE: Use a disposable makeup sponge to evenly apply a thin layer of paint to your sculptures.

ADDING COLOR TO CLAY

You can purchase air-dry clay in a variety of colors, but personally, I prefer to use acrylic paint to add color to white air-dry clay. This allows me to control the intensity of the color and create more realistic-looking succulents that display subtle shading. You'll see the necessary colors listed for each project—you can either buy pre-mixed colors or create your own.

1 Squeeze a dab of acrylic paint directly onto the clay. If you are using multiple colors, add a dab of each color to the clay.

2 Knead the clay between your fingers to incorporate the color into the clay.

3 This is how the clay should look when the color has been mixed in fully.

4 Cover any clay you don't plan to use immediately in plastic wrap.

TIPS

- In addition to acrylic paint, you can also use watercolor paint or watercolor pens to add color to clay.

- A little paint goes a long way! Add a little bit of paint at a time and knead it into the clay. Compare the color to the photo and add more paint if necessary—just remember, the color will appear darker when dry.

- If you add too much paint, add more clay to dilute the color.

- Mixing your own colored clay allows for more complex shades, but you can also use pre-packaged colored clay.

- Always remember to make the clay slightly lighter than you want the finished color as it will appear darker when it dries.

- A few of the projects in this book feature marbled clay where the color is intentionally left partially mixed. You'll see this noted in the materials list for the individual project instructions.

HOW TO USE THIS BOOK

1 The dimensions provided reference the size (width × depth × height) of the sculpture after it has dried.

2 When you see "clay" listed in the materials section, this means a 3:1 mixture of air-dry clay to lightweight air-dry clay (refer to page 52).

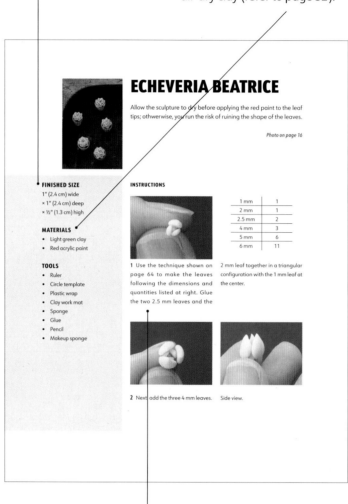

ECHEVERIA BEATRICE

Allow the sculpture to dry before applying the red paint to the leaf tips; othwerwise, you run the risk of ruining the shape of the leaves.

Photo on page 16

FINISHED SIZE
1" (2.4 cm) wide
× 1" (2.4 cm) deep
× ½" (1.3 cm) high

MATERIALS
• Light green clay
• Red acrylic paint

TOOLS
• Ruler
• Circle template
• Plastic wrap
• Clay work mat
• Sponge
• Glue
• Pencil
• Makeup sponge

INSTRUCTIONS

1 mm	1
2 mm	1
2.5 mm	2
4 mm	3
5 mm	6
6 mm	11

1 Use the technique shown on page 64 to make the leaves following the dimensions and quantities listed at right. Glue the two 2.5 mm leaves and the 2 mm leaf together in a triangular configuration with the 1 mm leaf at the center.

2 Next add the three 4 mm leaves.   Side view.

3 When dimensions are provided for leaves and other components, they indicate the diameter of the balls of clay to be formed prior to shaping, not the finished component. For example, a 2 mm leaf = a leaf made from a 2 mm ball of clay. You can use a ruler to measure the diameter, but a circle template makes the task much easier.

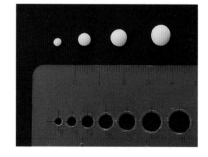

PROJECT INSTRUCTIONS

One of the most appealing things about crafting with air-dry clay is that you don't need lots of fancy tools or materials. By following the techniques illustrated in the project instructions, you'll be able to create realistic-looking clay succulents with your own hands!

SEDUM PACHYPHYLLUM

The sedum pachyphyllum uses all the basic clay succulent techniques, so it is a great project for beginners.

Photo on page 8

FINISHED SIZE

1" (2.5 cm) wide
× ¾" (2 cm) deep
× 1¾" (4.5 cm) high

MATERIALS

- Gray-green clay
- Yellow-green clay
- Red acrylic paint
- Sand-gray acrylic paint
- 22-gauge wire

TOOLS

- Ruler
- Circle template
- Clay work mat
- Plastic wrap
- Sponge
- Glue
- Diagonal cutting pliers
- Clay spatula
- Makeup sponge
- Paintbrush
- Flat-nose pliers

INSTRUCTIONS

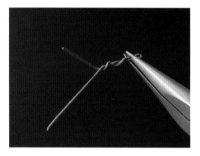

1 Cut a 2¾" (7 cm) piece of wire. Use flat-nose pliers to bend and twist the wire into a stem shape with one leg longer than the other. Squeeze the end to flatten the loop.

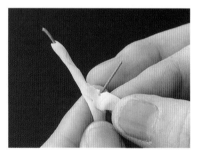

2 Wrap gray-green clay around the wire to make a stem about ¼" (7 mm) thick.

3 Use a clay spatula to make small indents along the stem.

4 Completed view of the stem.

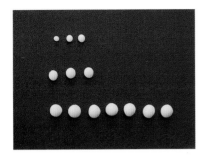

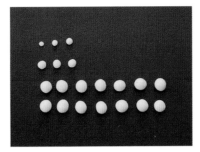

SMALLER BUD		
	1 mm	1
	2 mm	1
	3 mm	1
	3.5 mm	3
	4.5 mm	7-8

LARGER BUD		
	1 mm	1
	2 mm	1
	3 mm	1
	3.5 mm	3
	5 mm	14-15

5 To make leaves for the smaller bud, start by rolling balls of yellow-green clay following the dimensions and quantities listed at right.

To make the leaves for the larger bud, start by rolling balls of yellow-green clay following the dimensions and quantities listed at right.

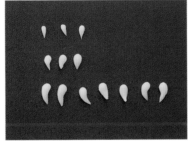

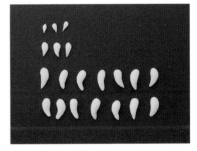

6 Roll each ball in the palm of your hand forming one pointed end to achieve the characteristic "jellybean" shape.

7 Completed view once all the leaves for the smaller bud have been formed into shape.

Completed view once all the leaves for the larger bud have been formed into shape. Let all leaves dry for at least 30 minutes.

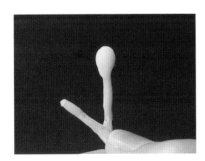

8 You'll start by attaching the leaves to the larger bud. Apply a dab of glue to one leg of the stem. Make a 4 mm ball of yellow-green clay and attach it to the glued area.

9 Apply glue to the pointed ends of the 1 mm, 2 mm, and 3 mm leaves from step 7 (for the larger bud). Attach these leaves to the stem in a triangular configuration.

10 Glue the 3.5 mm leaves to the stem, forming a triangle around the the leaves from step 9.

11 Glue the 5 mm leaves to the stem, filling the remaining space.

12 Follow the same process to glue the leaves to the other leg of the stem to create the smaller bud.

13 Apply some red paint to a makeup sponge.

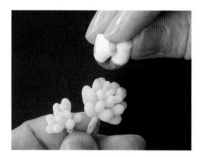

14 Dab the sponge to transfer the red paint to the tips of the leaves.

TIP If necessary, use a paper towel to remove excess paint from the sponge.

15 Completed view once the paint has been applied to the leaves. Add color gradually for a natural look.

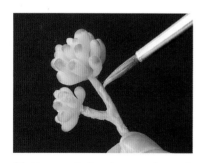

16 Use a paintbrush to apply sand-gray paint to the stem. Leave some areas unpainted for a realistic look.

17 Completed view. Once the paint is dry, gently bend the stem to adjust the shape.

View from the underside.

SEDUM RUBROTINCTUM

Use yellow-green and red clay to achieve the gradated coloration characteristic of this plant. For an even more realistic look, use a paintbrush to apply subtle red shading to the leaves.

Photo on page 9

FINISHED SIZE

⅝" (1.7 cm) wide
× ⅝" (1.7 cm) deep
× 2" (4.8 cm) high

MATERIALS

- Light brown clay
- Red clay
- Yellow-green clay
- Red acrylic paint
- Sand-gray acrylic paint
- 22-gauge wire

TOOLS

- Ruler
- Circle template
- Plastic wrap
- Clay work mat
- Sponge
- Glue
- Diagonal cutting pliers
- Clay spatula
- Paintbrush
- Flat-nose pliers

INSTRUCTIONS

1 Fold a 3½" (9 cm) piece of wire in half. Use flat-nose pliers to twist the wire around itself.

2 Wrap light brown clay around the wire to make a stem about ¼" (5 mm) thick. Use a clay spatula to make small indents along the stem.

3 Use the technique shown on page 59 to make the leaves with yellow-green and red clay following the dimensions and quantities listed at right.

YELLOW-GREEN	
1 mm	1
2 mm	1
3 mm	1
3.5 mm	3

RED	
4 mm	22-24

4 Apply a dab of glue to the stem. Make a 4 mm ball of red clay and attach it to the glued area.

5 Glue the 1 mm, 2 mm, and 3 mm yellow-green leaves to the stem in a triangular configuration. Next, glue the 3.5 mm yellow-green leaves to the stem forming a triangle around the first group of leaves. Finally, glue the 4 mm red leaves to the stem, filling in the remaining space.

6 Use a paintbrush to lightly apply red paint to the outer three yellow-green leaves.

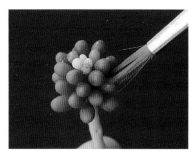

7 Apply a bit of red paint to the tips of the red leaves as well.

TIP Adding red paint to the red clay leaves creates a more complex texture.

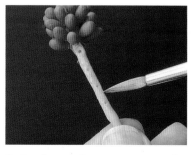

8 Apply sand-gray paint to the stem.

9 Completed view.

10 Once the paint is dry, gently bend the stem to create a subtly curved shape.

TIP To make a sedum rubrotinctum without a stem, adhere leaves to a 7 mm ball of red clay.

A NOTE ON STEMS

A toothpick works best for plants with straight stems, while wire should be used for plants with stems that will be bent, such as the sedum rubrotinctum shown here. 22-gauge wire should work well for most of the designs in this book, but thinner 30-gauge wire can also be used to create more delicate stems. If you plan to arrange your clay succulent sculpture on the surface of the soil, omit a stem and attach the leaves to a clay base as shown on the opposite page.

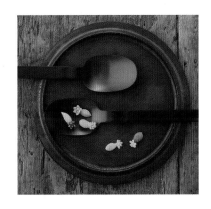

SEDUM LEAF CUTTINGS

These cute and colorful sedum leaf cuttings are a great way to use up leftover clay.

Photo on page 12

MATERIALS
- Assorted colors of clay

TOOLS
- Ruler
- Circle template
- Plastic wrap
- Clay work mat
- Sponge
- Glue

INSTRUCTIONS

1 Use the technique shown on page 59 to make several small leaves in assorted colors. Glue leaves of the same color together to form a bud.

2 Use the same technique to make large leaves in assorted colors. Glue the buds to the tips of the large leaves.

ECHEVERIA LAUI

Echeveria laui leaves are covered in a powdery coating called farina that helps protect succulents. The smooth air-dry clay replicates this texture extremely well, but you can add white paint for even more detail.

Photo on page 13

FINISHED SIZE

1" (2.5 cm) wide
× 1" (2.5 cm) deep
× ½" (1.3 cm) high

MATERIALS

- Light blue clay

TOOLS

- Ruler
- Circle template
- Plastic wrap
- Clay work mat
- Sponge
- Glue

INSTRUCTIONS

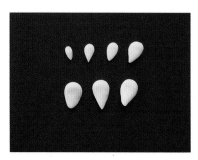

2 mm	1
2.5 mm	2
3 mm	1
5 mm	3

1 Use the technique shown on page 59 to make the leaves following the dimensions and quantities listed at right. Form the leaves into the shape shown in the photo above.

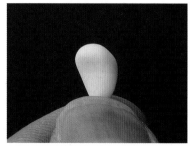

TIP Make a small indent at the center of each leaf.

2 Glue the two 2.5 mm leaves and the 3 mm leaf together in a triangular configuration with the 2 mm leaf at the center. Next, add the three 5 mm leaves.

3 Use the same process to make three 6 mm leaves and ten 7 mm leaves. Form them into the shape shown in the photo above with small points on the rounded ends.

4 Glue the leaves made in step 3 to the outside.

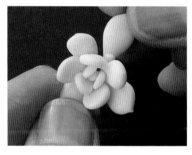

5 Pay attention to the overall balance as you add the rest of the leaves.

View from the underside.

6 Completed view.

SEDEVERIA SILVER FROST

Make sure to attach the leaves at an upward angle to replicate the look of a live sedeveria silver frost.

Photo on page 14

FINISHED SIZE

⅝" (1.7 cm) wide ×
⅝" (1.7 cm) deep ×
1¾" (4.5 cm) high

MATERIALS

- Yellow-green clay
- Red acrylic paint
- Toothpick

TOOLS

- Ruler
- Circle template
- Plastic wrap
- Clay work mat
- Makeup sponge
- Glue

INSTRUCTIONS

1 mm	1
2 mm	1
3 mm	2
4 mm	5
4.5 mm	20

1 Use the technique shown on page 59 to make the leaves following the dimensions and quantities listed at right. Form the leaves into the shape shown in the photo above. Let the leaves dry for 30 minutes.

2 Cut a toothpick in half. Apply a dab of glue to the cut end. Make a 4 mm ball of yellow-green clay and attach it to the glued area.

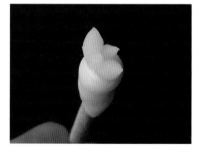

3 Glue the rounded ends of the 1 mm, 2 mm, and two 3 mm leaves to the stem. Make sure the pointed tips of the leaves face up.

4 Glue the 4 mm leaves to the stem in a star shape.

5 Randomly add the 4.5 mm leaves. This is the completed view after all the leaves have been attached.

TIP The leaves should angle upward. Make sure not to attach them horizontally.

6 Use a makeup sponge to dab red paint onto the tips of the leaves.

7 Completed view.

Side view.

GRAPTOPETALUM SHUUREI

This design features a straight stem made from a toothpick—it makes for a more secure base and is easier to make than a wire stem.

Photo on page 15

FINISHED SIZE

1" (2.3 cm) wide
× 1" (2.3 cm) deep
× 2" (5 cm) high

MATERIALS

- Blue clay
- Red clay
- Light brown clay
- Red acrylic paint
- Toothpick

TOOLS

- Ruler
- Circle template
- Plastic wrap
- Clay work mat
- Sponge
- Glue
- Paintbrush

INSTRUCTIONS

1 mm	1
2 mm	1
3 mm	1

1 Use the technique shown on page 64 to make the leaves from blue clay following the dimensions and quantities listed at right. Glue the leaves together in a triangular configuration.

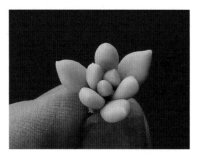

2 Use the same process to make three 4 mm leaves and three 5 mm leaves from blue clay. Glue these leaves to the outside.

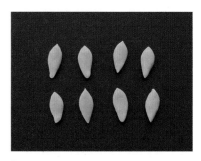

3 Make sixteen 6 mm leaves from red clay.

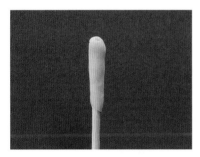

4 Cut a toothpick in half. Apply a dab of glue to the cut end. Make a 6 mm ball of light brown clay and attach it to the glued area.

5 Apply glue to the bottom of the piece from step 2 and attach it to the stem.

6 Glue the red leaves from step 3 to the outside.

7 Completed view after all the leaves have been attached and the sculpture has dried.

8 Use a paintbrush to lightly apply red paint to the outermost blue clay leaves and the red clay leaves.

9 Completed view.

ECHEVERIA BEATRICE

Allow the sculpture to dry before applying the red paint to the leaf tips; otherwise, you run the risk of ruining the shape of the leaves.

Photo on page 16

FINISHED SIZE

1" (2.4 cm) wide
× 1" (2.4 cm) deep
× ½" (1.3 cm) high

MATERIALS

- Light green clay
- Red acrylic paint

TOOLS

- Ruler
- Circle template
- Plastic wrap
- Clay work mat
- Sponge
- Glue
- Makeup sponge

INSTRUCTIONS

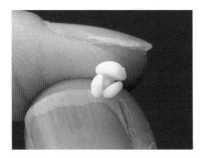

1 mm	1
2 mm	1
2.5 mm	2
4 mm	3
5 mm	6
6 mm	11

1 Use the technique shown on page 64 to make the leaves following the dimensions and quantities listed at right. Glue the two 2.5 mm leaves and the 2 mm leaf together in a triangular configuration with the 1 mm leaf at the center.

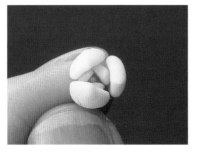

2 Next, add the three 4 mm leaves.   Side view.

3 Attach the remaining leaves, starting with the 5 mm ones and then finishing with the 6 mm leaves. Pay attention to the overall balance as you add the rest of the leaves.

4 Completed view once all the leaves have been attached.

5 Use a makeup sponge to apply a bit of red paint to the tips of the leaves.

6 Completed view.

TIP There are numerous varieties of echeveria Beatrice, so use different shades of green if you plan to display multiple in the same arrangement.

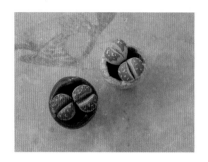

LITHOPS

Lithops are known for their vibrant coloring. We've used purple clay and light purple paint here, but green, orange, and red also work well.

Photo on page 17

FINISHED SIZE

⅜" (1 cm) wide
× ⅜" (8 mm) deep
× ⅝" (1.4 cm) high

MATERIALS

- Purple clay
- Light purple acrylic paint
- 22-gauge wire

TOOLS

- Ruler
- Circle template
- Plastic wrap
- Clay work mat
- Sponge
- Glue
- Diagonal cutting pliers
- Clay spatula
- Toothpick
- Paintbrush

INSTRUCTIONS

1 Cut a 1¼" (3 cm) piece of wire. Make a 1 cm ball of purple clay and glue it to the wire. Adjust to create an upside down pear shape.

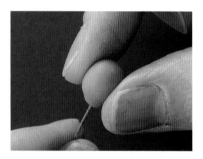

2 Gently squeeze to flatten the clay slightly.

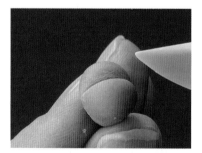

3 Use a clay spatula to make a shallow slice down the center. This should create a heart shape. Let the clay dry.

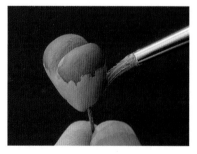

4 Apply light purple paint to the lower section and inside the sliced area.

5 Use a toothpick to add dots of light purple paint to the top. Use the toothpick to spread the dots of paint for a more natural look.

6 Completed view.

Side view.

TIP For green lithops, use green clay, and then apply light green paint.

Side view.

MONILARIA

Monilaria is renowned for its unique bunny-shaped silhouette. They are gregarious plants, so make several and arrange them together.

Photo on page 18

FINISHED SIZE

⅛" (4 mm) wide
× ⅛" (4 mm) deep
× ¾" (2 cm) high

MATERIALS

- Green clay
- Yellow-green clay
- Light brown clay
- White acrylic paint
- 22-gauge wire

TOOLS

- Ruler
- Circle template
- Plastic wrap
- Clay work mat
- Sponge
- Glue
- Diagonal cutting pliers
- Paintbrush
- Clay spatula

INSTRUCTIONS

1 Use the technique shown on page 59 to make two 2 mm leaves from green clay.

2 Cut a 1¼" (3 cm) piece of wire. Make a 6 mm ball of yellow-green clay and glue it to the wire. Use a clay spatula to make a shallow slice to create an uneven heart shape.

3 Glue the two leaves from step 1 to the heart-shaped clay. Make sure the rounded ends of the leaves point upward.

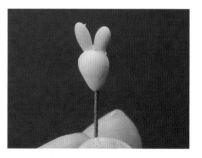

4 Completed view after attaching the leaves.

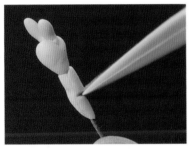

5 Apply glue to the wire. Make a 6 mm ball of light brown clay, then flatten it and wrap it around the wire. Use a clay spatula to score a line around the middle.

6 Completed view after making the line.

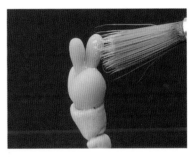

7 Add some white paint to a dry paintbrush and apply to the leaves.

8 Completed view.

CONOPHYTUM

Combine transparent clay with petals made from paper to capture the unique characteristics of this succulent. Make several and arrange densely for realistic-looking conophytum.

Photo on page 19

FINISHED SIZE

⅝" (1.5 cm) wide
× ⅜" (1 cm) deep
× 1¼" (3 cm) high

MATERIALS

- Transparent clay
- Varnish or sealer
- White clay
- Yellow-green clay
- Green, yellow, and red or pink acrylic paint
- 22-gauge wire
- Calligraphy paper or tissue paper

TOOLS

- Ruler
- Circle template
- Plastic wrap
- Clay work mat
- Sponge
- Glue
- Diagonal cutting pliers
- Scissors
- Paintbrush
- Clay spatula
- Toothpick
- Paintbrush

INSTRUCTIONS

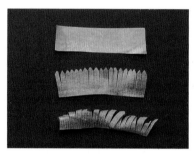

1 Use the process shown in steps 1-3 on page 72 to make a heart shape from a 1.5 cm ball of transparent clay. Insert a 1¼" (3 cm) piece of wire through the center so it extends out the top slightly. Let the clay dry a bit so the surface can be painted.

2 If your paper is white, paint it pink. Red paint was mixed with lots of water and applied to white calligraphy paper in the photo above, but you can also buy pink tissue paper. Once the paper is dry, cut a ⅜" × 1½" (1 × 3.5 cm) rectangle. Make slices into the paper every 1-2 mm, being careful not to cut all the way through the paper. Curl the cut paper as shown on page 77.

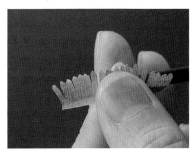

TIP Use a cylindrical object, like a paintbrush handle or chopstick to curl the cut paper.

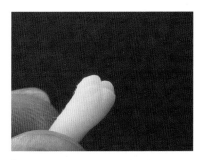

3 Roll a 3 mm ball of white clay into a cylinder, then make a cross-shaped indent at the tip.

4 Apply glue to the uncut base of the paper and wrap it around the white clay cylinder from step 3.

5 Completed view after the petals have been attached.

6 Form a 4 mm ball of yellow-green clay into a flat oval, and then cut a zigzag shape along the top, as shown in the photo above.

7 Apply glue to the base of the flower from step 5. Wrap the yellow-green clay from step 6 around the base. Smooth out the seam.

8 Use a paintbrush to apply green paint to the base of the leaf from step 1. Cover the lower section completely, then use a fine brush to add dots to the upper section. Leave the very top unpainted.

9 Completed view once the clay has been painted. Let dry for at least one day.

10 Apply a dab of glue to the tip of the wire that extends from the top of the leaf. Insert the base of the flower onto the wire.

11 Use a toothpick to apply dots of yellow paint to the center of the flower.

12 Completed view once the yellow paint has been added.

13 Apply varnish to the unpainted area to emphasize the translucent effect.

14 Completed view.

CRASSULA PELLUCIDA SUBSP. MARGINALIS

Green and white clay are wrapped together to create delicate, subtly shaded leaves. Take care not to rip the leaves when inserting the wire through the center—they're fragile.

Photo on page 20

FINISHED SIZE

¼" (5 mm) wide
× 1⁄16" (2 mm) deep
× 2¾" (7 cm) high

MATERIALS

- White clay
- Green clay
- Pink acrylic paint
- 30-gauge wire

TOOLS

- Ruler
- Circle template
- Plastic wrap
- Clay work mat
- Sponge
- Glue
- Diagonal cutting pliers
- Clay spatula
- Tweezers
- Toothpick

INSTRUCTIONS

1 Roll a 1.5 mm ball of white clay into a cylinder with pointed ends.

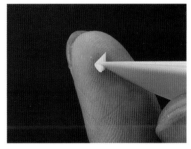

2 With the leaf from step 1 positioned on your fingertip, insert the tip of a clay spatula into the center and gently press to push the pointed ends upward. This will become the very topmost leaf.

3 Roll a bit of white clay into a cylinder. Next, roll a bit of green clay into a cylinder and position it on top of the white clay.

4 Wrap the clay cylinder from step 3 with a thin layer of white clay. Roll the cylinder out so it's about ¼" (4 mm) in diameter and both ends are pointed.

5 Use a clay spatula to cut five pieces about 1 mm thick.

6 Gently adjust the shape of the pieces so both ends are pointed.

7 Pinch the center of each piece with tweezers. This will divide each piece into a double leaf set.

8 Cut another piece from the cylinder that is slightly smaller than those from step 5.

9 Apply a dab of glue to the topmost leaf from step 2 and attach it to the leaf from step 8.

10 Cut a 2¾" (7 cm) piece of wire. Apply a dab of glue to the wire in the area you plan to position a set of leaves. Insert the wire through one of the double leaves from step 7. Make sure to insert the wire through the top of the leaf to avoid smearing the glue. Repeat process to attach all 5 double leaf sets.

11 Adjust the positions of the double leaves so they face different directions and are at different angles.

12 Apply a dab of glue to the tip of the wire and attach the piece from step 9.

13 Adjust the leaves so they point upward. Let dry.

14 Use a toothpick to apply dots of pink paint to the edges of the leaves.

15 Completed view.

ECHEVERIA WEST RAINBOW

To create the green and white shading on the leaves, make a striped pattern with the clay and then cut into individual leaves.

Photo on page 21

FINISHED SIZE

¾" (2 cm) wide
× ¾" (2 cm) deep
× ½" (1.2 cm) high

MATERIALS

- Green clay
- White clay
- Pink acrylic paint

TOOLS

- Ruler
- Circle template
- Plastic wrap
- Clay work mat
- Sponge
- Glue
- Clay spatula
- Paintbrush

INSTRUCTIONS

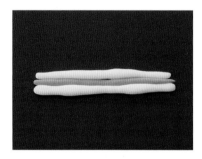

1 Roll two ⅛" (3 mm) diameter cylinders of white clay and one ⅛" (3 mm) diameter cylinder of green clay. Align as shown in the above photo.

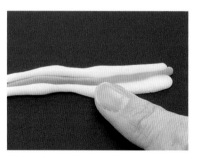

2 Use your finger to flatten and blend the clay together slightly.

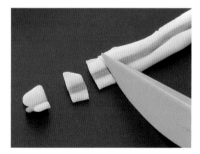

3 Use a clay spatula to cut into ¼" (5 mm) pieces.

4 Pinch the tip and form into a leaf shape. Repeat to make 11 leaves total.

5 Make small leaves using 1 mm, 2 mm, and 3 mm balls of white clay. Arrange the leaves in a bundle and adhere together at the bottom.

6 Use a 7 mm ball of white clay to make a base. Adhere the bundle of leaves from step 5 to the center of the base, then attach the leaves from step 4, starting at the center and working outward.

7 Make 10 leaves using 6 mm balls of green clay.

8 Add the green leaves to the piece from step 6.

9 Use a paintbrush to apply pink paint to the leaves. Make the color darker at the center and lighter toward the outside.

10 Completed view.

Side view.

ECHEVERIA CANTE

The echeveria cante displays a beautiful shade of light blue with striking pink accents. Use the instructions for the echeveria laui on page 64 as a reference for shaping the leaves.

Photo on page 22

FINISHED SIZE

1½" (4 cm) wide
× 1½" (4 cm) deep
× ⅝" (1.5 cm) high

MATERIALS

- Light blue clay
- Pink acrylic paint

TOOLS

- Ruler
- Circle template
- Plastic wrap
- Clay work mat
- Sponge
- Glue
- Makeup sponge

INSTRUCTIONS

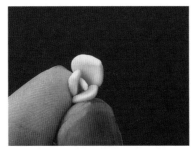

1 Use 1 mm, 2 mm, 3 mm, and 4 mm balls of light blue clay to make leaves, then bundle them together as shown on page 64.

2 Make two 5 mm leaves, three 6 mm leaves, and fifteen 7 mm leaves using light blue clay.

3 Attach the leaves to the piece from step 1.

4 View after all the leaves have been attached.

5 Use a makeup sponge to apply pink paint to the edges of the outer leaves.

6 Completed view.

FINISHED SIZE
1¼" (3 cm) wide
× ⅛" (3 mm) deep
× 2½" (6 cm) high

MATERIALS
- Green clay
- Purple clay
- Purple acrylic paint
- 30-gauge wire

TOOLS
- Ruler
- Circle template
- Plastic wrap
- Clay work mat
- Sponge
- Glue
- Diagonal cutting pliers
- Paintbrush

OTHONNA CAPENSIS

Use a wire core for the stem to create a plant with an adjustable shape.

Photo on page 23

INSTRUCTIONS

1 Cut 20 pieces of ¼" (5 mm) wire and paint them purple.

2 Make three 2 mm green leaves and seventeen 3 mm green leaves (refer to page 59). Apply a dab of glue to the end of each piece of wire and insert into a leaf.

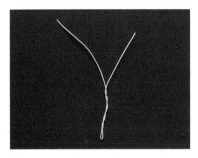

3 Cut a 4¾" (12 cm) piece of wire and twist it into shape as shown in the above photo.

4 Wrap the wire with purple clay.

5 Completed view after the wire has been wrapped in clay. Make a small branch using 1" (2.5 cm) of wire and wrap it in purple clay. Add a dab of glue, then attach it to the main stem.

6 Add dabs of glue the wires at the base of the leaves, and then insert into the purple stem.

7 View once all the leaves have been attached.

8 Apply purple paint to the leaves and stem.

9 Completed view. Gently bend the wire to adjust the shape as desired.

OROSTACHYS BOEHMERI

Use a metal ball stylus to form the uniquely round leaves characteristic of orostachys boehmeri.

Photo on page 24

FINISHED SIZE

2¼" (5.4 cm) wide
× 1" (2.5 cm) deep
× ¾" (2 cm) high

MATERIALS

- Light green clay
- 30-gauge wire

TOOLS

- Ruler
- Circle template
- Plastic wrap
- Clay work mat
- Sponge
- Glue
- Diagonal cutting pliers
- Ball stylus
- Clay spatula

INSTRUCTIONS

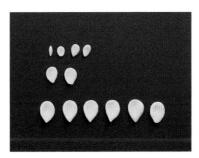

1 mm	1
2 mm	1
2.5 mm	2
3 mm	2
3.5 mm	6-7

1 Use the technique shown on page 64 to make the leaves following the dimensions and quantities listed at right.

TIP Use a ball stylus to give the leaves an even more pronounced round shape.

2 To make the stem, cover a 1¼" (3 cm) wire with clay. Make a 4 mm ball of clay and attach it to the tip of the wire.

3 Adhere the 1 mm leaf to the center of the stem. Add the 2 mm and 2.5 mm leaves in a triangular configuration and adhere with glue.

4 Add the remaining leaves from smallest to largest. This will be a new bud. Repeat steps 1-4 to make another new bud.

5 Next, make a mature bud. Make a 5 mm ball of clay and score with three lines.

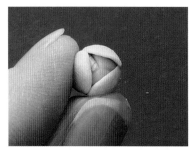

6 Follow the same process used in step 1 to make three 4 mm leaves and ten 5 mm leaves. Wrap the 4 mm leaves around the ball from step 5 and adhere with glue.

Side view.

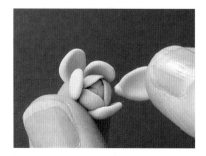

7 Use glue to attach the remaining leaves.

8 View once all the leaves have been attached to the mature bud.

9 Apply dabs of glue to the stems of the new bulbs and adhere to the center back of the mature bud.

Completed view.

HAWORTHIA 1

The haworthia shown here is green, but you can also use purple or brown paint. If possible, use transparent clay to capture the unique luster of this plant.

Photo on page 25

FINISHED SIZE

1¾" (4.5 cm) wide
× 1¾" (4.5 cm) deep
× 1" (2.5 cm) high

MATERIALS

- Transparent clay
- Varnish or sealer
- Green and yellow-green acrylic paint
- 30-gauge wire

TOOLS

- Ruler
- Circle template
- Plastic wrap
- Clay work mat
- Sponge
- Glue
- Diagonal cutting pliers
- Paintbrush

INSTRUCTIONS

4 mm	1
5 mm	1
6 mm	1
8 mm	3

1 Use the technique shown on page 64 to make the leaves following the dimensions and quantities listed at right.

2 Wrap a 12 mm ball of clay around a ¼" (7 mm) wire and form into a leaf shape as shown in the above photo. Repeat to make 22–25 leaves.

3 Start painting the leaves before the clay dries. Apply the green and yellow-green paint to the base of the leaves.

4 Insert the wires into a sponge and allow the paint to dry (arrange the leaves without wires on top of the sponge).

5 Make a base using a slightly flattened 14 mm ball of clay. Use glue to adhere the 4 mm, 5 mm, and 6 mm leaves to the base.

6 Arrange the leaves densely, from smallest to largest. Stand 8 middle leaves up vertically, then attach the outer leaves so they are slightly angled sideways.

TIP Push the leaves toward the center to keep them densely packed.

7 Adjust the shape by pressing down on a couple of the outer leaves.

8 View once all the leaves have been attached.

9 Transparent clay can take up to two weeks to dry fully. It will shrink 20% when it dries.

10 Add varnish to increase the shine.

When using transparent clay, make sure you knead it well and make sure that you do not have any grease, such as lotion, on your hands. Note that larger pieces take longer to dry.

Center is slightly indented. Leaves are gathered densely.

HAWORTHIA 2

Plump dark green leaves are the characteristic feature of this plant. Use white acrylic paint to add subtle spots.

Photo on page 27

FINISHED SIZE

1¾" (4.5 cm) wide
× 1¾" (4.5 cm) deep
× ½" (1.3 cm) high

MATERIALS

- Transparent clay
- Varnish or sealer
- Dark green and white acrylic paint
- 30-gauge wire

TOOLS

- Ruler
- Circle template
- Plastic wrap
- Clay work mat
- Sponge
- Glue
- Diagonal cutting pliers
- Paintbrush
- Toothpick

INSTRUCTIONS

3 mm	1
5 mm	2
8 mm	3
12 mm	12

1 Use the technique shown on page 64 to make the leaves following the dimensions and quantities listed at right. Insert wire into the 8 mm and 12 mm leaves.

TIP Overhead view. Make the leaves triangular in shape.

2 Paint the leaves dark green, leaving the upper tip white.

3 Use a toothpick to apply spots of white paint to both the painted and unpainted areas of the leaves.

4 Attach the leaves to a base as shown on page 90. Once the clay dries, apply varnish.

A CLOSER LOOK
OVERHEAD VIEW

Triangular shaped leaves are a characteristic feature of this plant.

HAWORTHIA 3

Use tweezers to form the small spines along the edges of the leaves. Use the instructions for haworthia 1 on page 89 as a reference for the construction method.

Photo on page 27

FINISHED SIZE

2¼" (5.5 cm) wide
× 2¼" (5.5 cm) deep
× ¾" (2 cm) high

MATERIALS

- Transparent clay
- Varnish or sealer
- Green and yellow-green acrylic paint
- 30-gauge wire

TOOLS

- Ruler
- Circle template
- Plastic wrap
- Clay work mat
- Sponge
- Glue
- Diagonal cutting pliers
- Paintbrush
- Tweezers

INSTRUCTIONS

2 mm	1
3mm	1
5 mm	1
6 mm	1
7 mm	3
10 mm	12-14

1 Use the technique shown on page 64 to make the leaves following the dimensions and quantities listed at right.

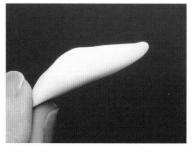

TIP Side view. Make the leaves thicker in the middle. Note: Use the side with the "corner" as the wrong side.

2 Pinch the leaves with tweezers to form small spines along the outer edges.

3 View after forming the spines.

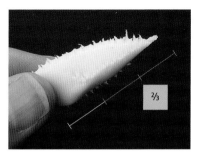

TIP Do not add spines along the lower ⅓ of the leaves.

4 Apply yellow-green paint to the rounded base, then add green lines to the entire leaf. This is the view from the right side of the leaf.

TIP View from the wrong side of the leaf. Make sure to apply paint to both sides.

5 Attach the leaves to a base, as shown on page 90. Once the clay dries, apply varnish.

A CLOSER LOOK

OVERHEAD VIEW
Use tweezers to make small spines along the edges of each leaf.

DETAIL
Paint the bottom ⅓ of each leaf yellow-green. Use green paint to draw thin lines from the bottom to the tip of each leaf.

SIDE VIEW
Haworthia display a variety of colors and shapes, plus some have spines while others don't. Use the construction techniques shown on pages 89-95 to create your own unique haworthia.

HYDROPONICS

Transform any succulent, such as the haworthia from page 89, into a hydroponic version by attaching roots to the bottom.

Photo on page 26

FINISHED SIZE

⅝" (1.5 cm) wide
× ⅝" (1.5 cm) deep
× 1¾" (4.5 cm) high

MATERIALS

- Light brown clay

TOOLS

- Ruler
- Circle template
- Plastic wrap
- Clay work mat
- Sponge
- Glue

INSTRUCTIONS

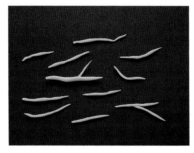

1 Roll pieces of light brown clay into long, thin cylinders. For reference, the longest one shown here measures about 2½" (6 cm).

2 Bundle the tips together and adhere with glue.

3 Completed view of the root bundle.

A CLOSER LOOK
SIDE VIEW

Hydroponic roots work best for plants with a flat base, such as haworthia or agave.

Include a few split roots for a more realistic look.

COPIAPOA

Use black clay for the thick spines at the top and black broom bristles for the thin spines along the sides of the cactus.

Photo on page 29

FINISHED SIZE

¾" (2 cm) wide
× ⅝" (1.5 cm) deep
× 1¼" (3 cm) high

MATERIALS

- Black clay
- Light green and white marbled clay
- Liquid clay
- Brown and beige acrylic paint
- 22-gauge wire
- Black broom bristles

TOOLS

- Ruler
- Circle template
- Plastic wrap
- Clay work mat
- Sponge
- Glue
- Diagonal cutting pliers
- Scissors
- Clay spatula
- Toothpick

INSTRUCTIONS

1 Use 1 mm balls of black clay to create long, thin cylinders for the spines. Let them dry completely.

2 Cut broom bristles into ¼" (7 mm) pieces. You'll need about 100 pieces.

3 Look for a broom with stiff, black bristles. A dustpan broom will work well.

4 Make an 18 mm ball of light green and white marbled clay.

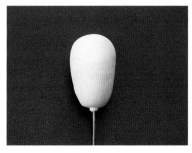

5 Cut a 1¼" (3 cm) piece of wire. Apply glue to the tip then adhere the 18 mm ball of clay. Adjust into an oval shape.

6 Use a clay spatula to score three lines, dividing the oval into equal segments.

7 Add two more lines in between each of the three existing lines. This will create a total of 9 lines.

8 Use your fingers to pinch the clay between each line and form ridges.

9 View after ridges have been formed.

10 Apply a dab of glue to the base of each of the clay spines and then insert into the top.

11 View after 20 clay spines have been inserted.

12 Apply a dab of glue to the base of each broom bristle spine and insert into the ridges in sets of two.

13 View after broom bristle spines have been inserted. Do not insert spines at the base as paint will be applied later.

14 Make a smaller bulb using a 7 mm ball of light green marbled clay and a ⅜" (1 cm) piece of wire. Score 6 lines onto the bulb and then insert spines as desired.

15 Apply a dab of glue to the wire and insert the smaller bulb into the larger one.

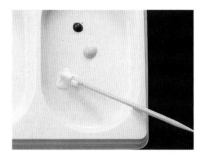

16 Apply a dab of liquid clay onto a palette. Mix in brown and beige paint, leaving the color marbled.

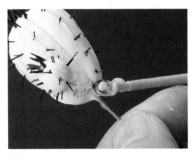

17 Use a toothpick to apply the paint to the base of the larger bulb.

18 Completed view.

A CLOSER LOOK
SIDE VIEW

Position the sets of bristle spines in a V-shape when inserting them into the cactus.

OPUNTIA

This is a great project for beginners! Use liquid clay to create the three-dimensional dot pattern.

Photo on page 30

Photo on page 30

FINISHED SIZE

1½" (3.5 cm) wide
× ¼" (5 mm) deep
× 2" (5 cm) high

MATERIALS

- Green clay
- Liquid clay
- White and brown acrylic paint
- 22-gauge wire
- 30-gauge wire

TOOLS

- Ruler
- Circle template
- Plastic wrap
- Clay work mat
- Sponge
- Glue
- Diagonal cutting pliers
- Clay spatula
- Toothpick

INSTRUCTIONS

1 Form 4 mm, 5 mm, and 6 mm balls of green clay into bean shapes. These will be the new paddles.

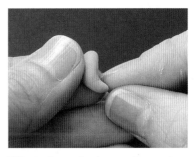

TIP To form the bean shape, first make a shape, then bend and squeeze the tip.

2 Insert ⅜" (1 cm) pieces of 30-gauge wire into the base of each paddle and let them dry.

3 Roll an 18 mm ball of green clay into a cylinder to form the main part of the cactus. Flatten it slightly.

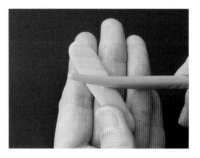

4 Use a clay spatula to lightly score a checkered patterned.

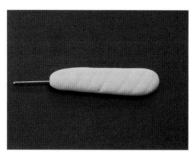

5 View after the pattern has been scored. Apply a dab of glue to a 1¼" (3 cm) piece of 22-gauge wire and insert it into the base.

6 Apply dabs of glue to the wires and insert the new paddles into the main part of the cactus.

7 Mix the white and brown paint into the liquid clay. Use a toothpick to apply dots of this mixture to the cactus. Use the scored checkered pattern as a guide when applying the dots.

8 Completed view.

ASTROPHYTUM ASTERIAS

This project incorporates a variety of techniques to capture the plants unique features, including the fuzzy top, three-dimensional dots, and white spotted pattern.

Photo on page 31

FINISHED SIZE

⅝" (1.7 cm) wide
× ⅝" (1.7 cm) deep
× ¾" (2 cm) high

MATERIALS

- Dark green clay
- Liquid clay
- White acrylic paint
- 22-gauge wire
- Facial tissue

TOOLS

- Ruler
- Circle template
- Plastic wrap
- Clay work mat
- Sponge
- Glue
- Diagonal cutting pliers
- Clay spatula
- Toothpick

INSTRUCTIONS

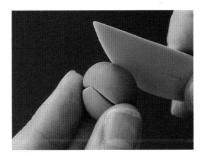

1 Form an 18 mm ball of clay. Use a clay spatula to score three lines, dividing the ball into equal segments.

2 Add one more line in between each of the three existing lines. This will create a total of 6 lines.

3 Apply a dab of glue to a 1¼" (3 cm) piece of wire, and then insert into the ball.

4 Tear a small piece of facial tissue.

5 Apply a dab of glue to the facial tissue and form it into a ball. Adhere to the top center of the clay ball.

6 Mix the liquid clay and white paint together. Use a toothpick to apply three-dimensional dots to the cactus as shown in the above photo.

7 View after dot pattern has been applied.

8 Use a toothpick to apply dots of white paint to the cactus. Add dots next to the scored lines and around the three-dimensional dots from step 7.

9 Completed view.

TILLANDSIA 1

Focus on the thin, airy silhouette of the individual leaves as you sculpt this plant. Make sure to form the leaves into shape before the clay dries.

Photo on page 35

FINISHED SIZE

2" (5 cm) wide
× 2" (5 cm) deep
× 1½" (4 cm) high

MATERIALS

- Light green clay

TOOLS

- Ruler
- Circle template
- Plastic wrap
- Clay work mat
- Sponge
- Glue
- Clay spatula

INSTRUCTIONS

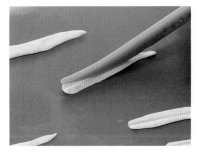

1 Flatten balls of clay into long, thin leaves about ¼" (5 mm) thick. Use a clay spatula to score a line down the center of each leaf. Make about 30 leaves total.

TIP Vary the length of the leaves for a more natural look. The leaves shown here measure about ⅜" (1 cm) for the smaller ones and 2½" (6 cm) for the larger ones. For an even more realistic look, use a slightly different shade of green for the 10 lower leaves to add dimension.

2 Add a dab of glue to the base of each smaller leaf and form into a bundle.

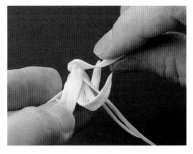

3 When attaching additional leaves, glue them to the bottom of the plant.

TIP Fan the leaves out as you work.

4 View after 20 leaves have been attached.

5 View after all 30 leaves have been attached.

6 Curl the leaves back so the plant forms a rounded shaped. Let dry.

View from the wrong side.

TILLANDSIA 2

Use the instructions for tillandsia 1 on page 105 as a reference for the construction method.

Photo on page 35

FINISHED SIZE

1¾" (4.5 cm) wide
× 1" (2.5 cm) deep
× 2¼" (5.5 cm) high

MATERIALS

- Green clay
- White acrylic paint

TOOLS

- Ruler
- Circle template
- Plastic wrap
- Clay work mat
- Sponge
- Glue
- Paintbrush

INSTRUCTIONS

1 Make nine 1¼"-2½" (3-6 cm) long pointed leaves. Gently squeeze the root areas to flatten.

2 Glue the leaves together following the process shown on page 105. Use a paintbrush to apply white paint to the roots. For best results, don't add water to the paint.

3 Completed view.

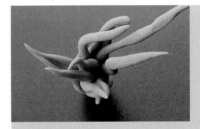

A CLOSER LOOK
SIDE VIEW
Arrange the leaves before the clay dries. Try bending some leaves while leaving others straight. In addition to applying paint to the roots, you can also apply it to the surface of the leaves, just make sure to use a light touch.

TILLANDSIA 3

Use the instructions for tillandsia 1 on page 105 as a reference for the construction method.

Photo on page 35

FINISHED SIZE

1¾" (4.5 cm) wide
× 1¾" (4.5 cm) deep
× 1¼" (3 cm) high

MATERIALS

• Yellow-green clay

TOOLS

• Ruler
• Circle template
• Plastic wrap
• Clay work mat
• Sponge
• Glue
• Clay spatula

INSTRUCTIONS

1 Make 38 leaves that measure ⅛" (3 mm) wide × ⅜"-1½" (1-4 cm) long. Glue the leaves together following the process shown on page 105.

TIP The leaves are thin, so take care to only apply glue to the tips.

3 Curve the leaves into shape before the clay dries.

A CLOSER LOOK
OVERHEAD VIEW

SIDE VIEW

Attach leaves so they radiate out.

Vary the length of the leaves for a natural look. Add a few smaller leaves to the roots. Apply undiluted white paint to the roots for an even more realistic look.

DYCKIA

Use pinking shears to create a zigzag pattern along the leaf edges. Mixing air-dry clay and lightweight air-dry clay in a 1:1 ratio produces a clay with a springy texture that is easier to cut with scissors.

Photo on page 38

FINISHED SIZE

3⅛" (8 cm) wide
× 3⅛" (8 cm) deep
× 1¼" (3 cm) high

MATERIALS

- White clay (1:1 ratio of air dry clay and lightweight air dry clay)
- Red, dark brown, and ochre acrylic paint

TOOLS

- Ruler
- Circle template
- Plastic wrap
- Clay work mat
- Sponge
- Glue
- Rolling pin
- Pinking shears (with 2 mm teeth)
- Paintbrush

INSTRUCTIONS

1 Mix the clays in a 1:1 ratio. Use a rolling pin to spread out the clay until it is about 1 mm thick.

2 Use pinking shears to cut triangular-shaped leaves.

3 Make about 35 leaves of varying length. The longest leaf should measure about 2¾" (7 cm).

4 Combine the red, dark brown, and ochre paint to produce an unevenly mixed maroon color.

5 Paint the center of each leaf, leaving the zigzag edges white.

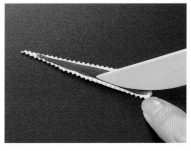

6 Once the paint has dried, use a clay spatula to apply pressure to the edges of the leaves until they curl upward.

7 Bend each leaf so it curls backward.

8 Glue a few smaller leaves together in a bundle so the painted surfaces point upward.

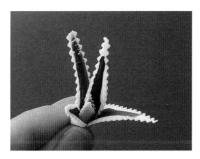

TIP Continue pressing the leaves into a bundle as you attach additional ones at the base.

9 Attach each leaf a little lower than the previous one.

10 As you attach additional leaves, they will naturally fan out.

11 View once all the leaves have been attached.

12 Insert the succulent face down into a cup while it dries. The cup will give the succulent a rounded shape.

Completed view.

Side view.

A CLOSER LOOK
OVERHEAD VIEW

A mixture of air-dry clay and lightweight air-dry clay produces a paper-like texture that's easier to cut with scissors.

Position a couple of leaves upright at the center, and then spread the rest of the leaves out in a radiating pattern. Think of the shape of a pineapple's crown as you attach the leaves.

Leaving the paint slightly unmixed will produce more natural looking color with subtle shading and variation.

PACHYPODIUM

Pachypodium's tuberous roots are not perfect spheres, but rather irregular ovals. Leave the clay slightly unmixed to create a marbled appearance perfect for the roots.

Photo on page 40

Photo on page 40

FINISHED SIZE

1½" (4 cm) wide
× 1¼" (3 cm) deep
× 2" (5 cm) high

MATERIALS

- Sand gray and white marbled clay
- Light green clay
- 22-gauge wire
- 30-gauge wire
- Scrub brush

TOOLS

- Ruler
- Circle template
- Plastic wrap
- Clay work mat
- Sponge
- Glue
- Diagonal cutting pliers
- Scissors
- Clay spatula

INSTRUCTIONS

1 Form 1.5 mm balls of light green clay into long, flat leaves, and then insert ¼" (7 mm) pieces of wire. Make 21 of these leaves.

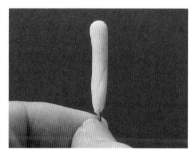

2 Wrap a 6 mm ball of sand gray and white marbled clay around a 1" (2.5 cm) piece of wire.

3 Apply dabs of glue and insert a handful of leaves into the top of the root from step 2.

4 Cut bristles from a scrub brush to use as spines. The spines should measure about ⅛" (3 mm) long.

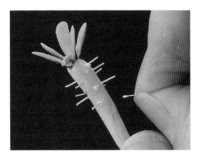

5 Apply glue to the base of each spine and insert into the root. Insert the spines into the top half of the root only.

6 Follow the same process to make two more roots. Make one of the roots V-shaped and the other straight.

7 Form a 20 mm ball of sand gray and white marbled clay into an egg shape.

8 Apply a dab of glue to a 1¼" (3 cm) wire and insert into the base of the egg. Apply glue to the base of the roots from step 6 and insert into the top of the egg.

9 Use a clay spatula to blend the clay around the base of the roots, making sure no wire is exposed.

10 Use a clay spatula to lightly score lines into the egg shape.

11 Completed view.

TIP Leaves can also grow directly from the tuberous root. Add a few wrinkles to the root at the base of the leaves for a realistic look.

DIONAEA MUSCIPULA

Dionaea muscipula, also known as the Venus flytrap, possess some very unique features, including spiky "teeth" and long, wavy stems. Use scissors and tweezers to carefully form these special details.

Photo on page 41

FINISHED SIZE

1" (2.5 cm) wide
× ⅜" (8 mm) deep
× 2½" (6 cm) high

MATERIALS

- White clay
- Yellow-green clay
- Red and green acrylic paint
- 30-gauge wire

TOOLS

- Ruler
- Circle template
- Plastic wrap
- Clay work mat
- Sponge
- Glue
- Diagonal cutting pliers
- Scissors
- Tweezers
- Paintbrush

INSTRUCTIONS

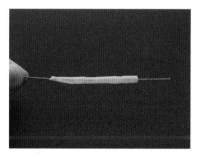

1 Wrap a 5 mm ball of yellow-green clay around the center of a 3⅛" (8 cm) piece of wire. Leave ⅝" (1.5 cm) of wire exposed at both ends. Flatten the clay slightly.

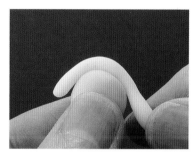

2 Roll a 6 mm ball of white clay out into a thin cylinder. Wrap the cylinder around a 9 mm ball of yellow-green clay.

3 Flatten the piece from step 2 until it is about 1 mm thick.

4 Flatten the white area even more until it is about 0.5 mm thick.

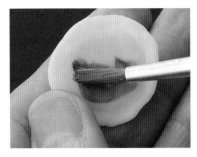

5 Use a paintbrush to apply red paint to the center, leaving a bit of the yellow-green clay visible around the edges.

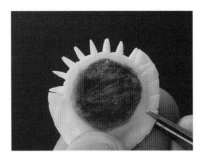

6 Use scissors to cut V-shaped notches out of the white clay.

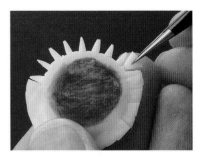

7 Use tweezers to carefully remove the excess clay from the cut areas.

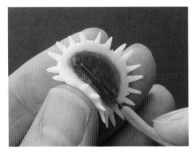

8 Wrap the piece from step 5 around the exposed wire of the stem from step 1.

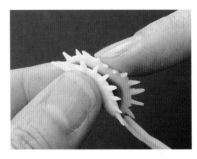

9 Fold the teeth in toward the center.

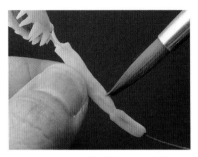

10 Paint the back of the stem green.

11 Apply green paint around the edges on the back of the head.

12 Make additional stems as desired.

PLATYCERIUM

Use a piece of cork as the foundation for the platycerium. You can even add wire and hang the sculpture on the wall.

Photo on page 42

INSTRUCTIONS

1 Roll the green clay out until it is about 0.5-1 mm thick. Cut four large leaves of varying shapes and four small leaves. Wrap the large leaves around pieces of wire as shown at right. The large leaves measure about 1½" (4 cm).

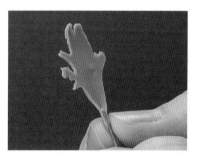

2 Gently wrap the base of the larger leaves around the wire.

3 Roll the light brown clay out as thin as possible. Tear it into pieces as shown in the above photo. Use a clay spatula to score lines for added texture. For an even more realistic look, use a slightly different shade of light brown for a couple of the pieces.

4 Cut the cork in half. Use an awl to puncture two holes close to the top on the flat side. The holes should not extend all the way through the cork. These will be used to insert wire for hanging.

5 Fold a 2½" (6 cm) piece of wire in half. Apply glue to the ends and insert into the holes in the cork. Note: Dark brown wire is used here.

6 Use glue to adhere a 10 mm ball of light brown clay to the front of the cork. Flatten the clay slightly. This will be the foundation for the plant.

7 Apply glue to the bases of the pieces of light brown clay from step 3. Adhere the pieces to the foundation to create the bulb.

8 View after all the pieces have been attached.

Top view.

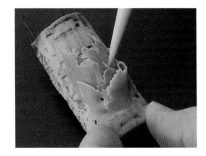

9 Use a clay spatula to puncture two holes. Position one hole at the middle right (shown above) and one hole at the bottom left.

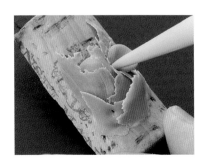

10 Apply a dab of glue to the middle right hole and insert one of the small leaves without wires from step 1.

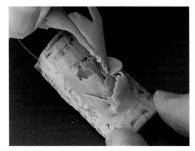

11 Apply glue to the bases of the four leaves with wire from step 1. Insert into the middle right hole on top of the smaller leaf.

12 View after the four leaves with wire have been attached. Make sure to spread the leaves out in different directions.

13 Insert the remaining three small leaves without wires into the bottom left hole.

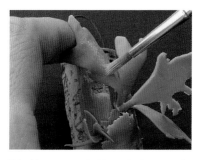

14 Use a paintbrush to apply undiluted white paint to the leaves. This will replicate the dried, powdery texture of the plant.

15 Apply brown paint to the tip of the bulb.

16 Completed view.

AGAVE

Sharp red spines provide a striking contrast to marbled green and white leaves.

Photo on page 43

FINISHED SIZE
2" (5 cm) wide
× 2" (5 cm) deep
× 1½" (3 .5 cm) high

MATERIALS
- White clay
- Red clay
- Green clay
- Red and dark brown acrylic paint

TOOLS
- Ruler
- Circle template
- Plastic wrap
- Clay work mat
- Sponge
- Glue
- Paintbrush

INSTRUCTIONS

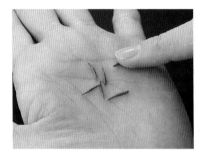

1 Roll 1.5 mm balls of red clay into small cylinders to make 13 spines.

2 Mix the green and white clay to form a marbled pattern.

3 Use 6 mm and 8 mm balls of marbled clay to make leaves with five pointed corners.

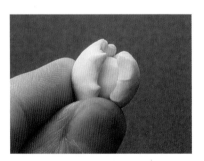

4 Make a 7 mm ball of white clay. Wrap the two leaves from step 3 around the ball and adhere with glue.

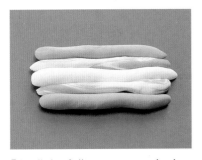

5 Roll the following into cylinders and align as shown in the above photo: two 7 mm balls of green clay, two 4 mm balls of marbled clay, and one 7 mm ball of white clay.

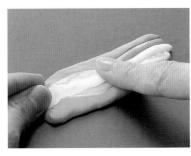

6 Flatten the cylinder and blend the colors. Repeat this process on the wrong side as well.

7 View once the clay has been blended. The piece should measure about 1¼" (3 cm) wide.

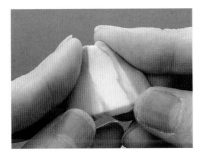

8 Cut the piece from step 7 into leaves following the dimensions and quantities listed at right. Form the leaves into a triangular shape by pushing on the edges.

5 mm	2
1 cm	2
1.5 cm	1
2 cm	7

9 Apply dabs of glue to the tips of the spines and insert into the pointed ends of the leaves.

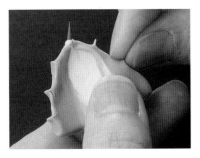

10 Pinch the edges of the leaves to form spikes.

11 Glue the leaves together into a bundle, starting with the smaller ones at the center.

TIP Make sure the spines point up.

12 Once all the leaves are attached, add red and dark brown paint on the tips of spines. Apply the paint unevenly.

13 Completed view.

A CLOSER LOOK
OVERHEAD VIEW

Adding dark brown paint to the tips of the spines creates a more realistic look.

BLACK-SPINED AGAVE

Black spines at the tips of the leaves serve as the namesake for this pretty plant.

Photo on page 44

FINISHED SIZE

2½" (6 cm) wide
× 2½" (6 cm) deep
× 1¼" (3 cm) high

MATERIALS

- Black clay
- Light blue-green clay
- Liquid clay
- White and dark brown acrylic paint
- 30-gauge wire

TOOLS

- Ruler
- Circle template
- Plastic wrap
- Clay work mat
- Sponge
- Glue
- Diagonal cutting pliers
- Toothpick
- Paintbrush

INSTRUCTIONS

1 Roll 1 mm balls of black clay into small cylinders to make 33 spines. Let dry.

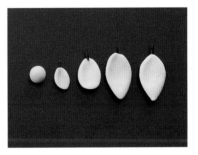

2 Make a 6 mm ball of light blue-green clay. Next, form leaves using a 4 mm, 6 mm, and two 7 mm balls of clay. Insert black spines into the tips of the four leaves.

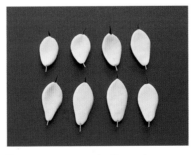

3 Form six 8 mm balls and twenty-three 10 mm balls of light blue-green clay into leaves. Insert black spines into the tips and pieces of wire into the bases. Let dry overnight.

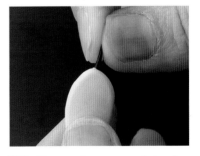

TIP The spines need to be completely dry before being inserted into the leaves. Otherwise, they will become misshapen.

4 Glue the 4 mm, 6 mm, and two 7 mm leaves from step 2 around the ball of clay.

5 Form a 5 mm ball of light blue-green clay into a mountain shape and apply a dab of glue to the top. Attach the piece from step 4.

6 Use glue to attach the six 8 mm leaves from step 3. Make sure the spines are pointing upward.

Side view.

7 Add the remaining leaves. Position the outer leaves so they stick out sideways.

8 Mix the dark brown paint with liquid clay. Use a toothpick to apply three-dimensional dots of this mixture to the edges of the leaves. Let dry.

9 Use a paintbrush to apply undiluted white paint to the leaves.

10 Completed view.

HOW TO MAKE A POT

Use plasticine to recreate the traditional unglazed pottery look.

Photo on page 31

FINISHED SIZE

1" (2.5 cm) wide
× 1" (2.5 cm) deep
× 1" (2.3 cm) high

MATERIALS

- Plasticine
- Red, brown, and white acrylic paint

TOOLS

- Ruler
- Circle template
- Plastic wrap
- Clay work mat
- Sponge
- Glue
- Rolling pin
- Clay spatula
- Pencil
- Scissors
- Paintbrush

INSTRUCTIONS

1 Use a rolling pin to spread the plasticine out until it's 1-1.5 mm thick.

2 Use a clay spatula to cut the templates from page 126 out of the plasticine.

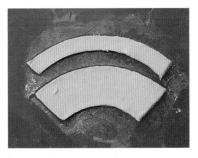

3 Completed view of cut pieces.

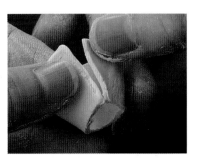

4 Apply glue to the edges of the larger piece and adhere them together.

5 Completed view after adhering.

6 Wrap the smaller piece around the top and adhere with glue.

7 Let dry.

8 Position the pot on top of your work surface. Insert small amount of plasticine inside and push it down to create the bottom.

9 Let the pot dry completely.

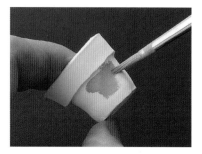

10 Mix the paint to create a terracotta color. Use a paintbrush to apply the paint to the pot.

11 Let the paint dry.

TEMPLATES

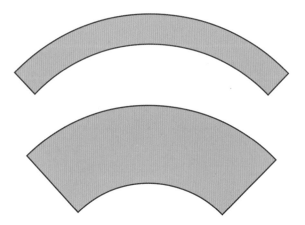

DISPLAY IDEAS

After all the time and effort that goes into sculpting clay succulents, it's important that the pots and other containers you use for display also look realistic. You can use your leftover clay to sculpt your own pots, or use store-bought containers. You can also add sand and soil to increase the realistic effect. Use the following tips for arranging your clay succulent displays.

ARRANGE IN A CLUSTER

Fill the container with a sponge or piece of clay, and then cover it with sand.

ADD STRUCTURE AND SUPPORT

Twist wires together before planting your clay succulents—this will provide stability and prevent your sculptures from falling over.

CREATE DECORATIVE POTTERY

Use leftover clay to create unique pots and containers. Add color and design elements like dots, lines, and shading.

USE NATURAL MATERIALS

Try using straw or raffia as a base for cacti.

BUY PRE-MADE CONTAINERS

You can purchase pre-made containers at dollhouse and miniature supply stores.

OBSERVE REFERENCES

When arranging your plants in a container, think about the direction that they'd grow. Use photos or real succulents as a reference.

RESOURCES

BLICK

www.dickblick.com

Art supply store with air-dry clay, sculpting tools, acrylic paint, varnishes and sealers

ETSY

www.etsy.com

Online marketplace with retailers selling Japanese air-dry clay such as Grace and Modena brand

HOBBY LOBBY

www.hobbylobby.com

National craft supply chain offering air-dry clay, sculpting tools, acrylic paint, varnishes and sealers

JOANN

www.joann.com

National craft supply chain offering air-dry clay, sculpting tools, acrylic paint, varnishes and sealers

MICHAEL'S

www.michaels.com

National craft supply chain offering air-dry clay, sculpting tools, acrylic paint, varnishes and sealers

RAINBOW RESOURCE CENTER

www.rainbowresource.com

Educational supplier offering an assortment of air-dry clay and modeling tools

SWEET PEA DOLLS

www.sweetpeadolls.co.uk

British site specializing in Japanese air-dry clay, including Sukerukun transparent air-dry clay